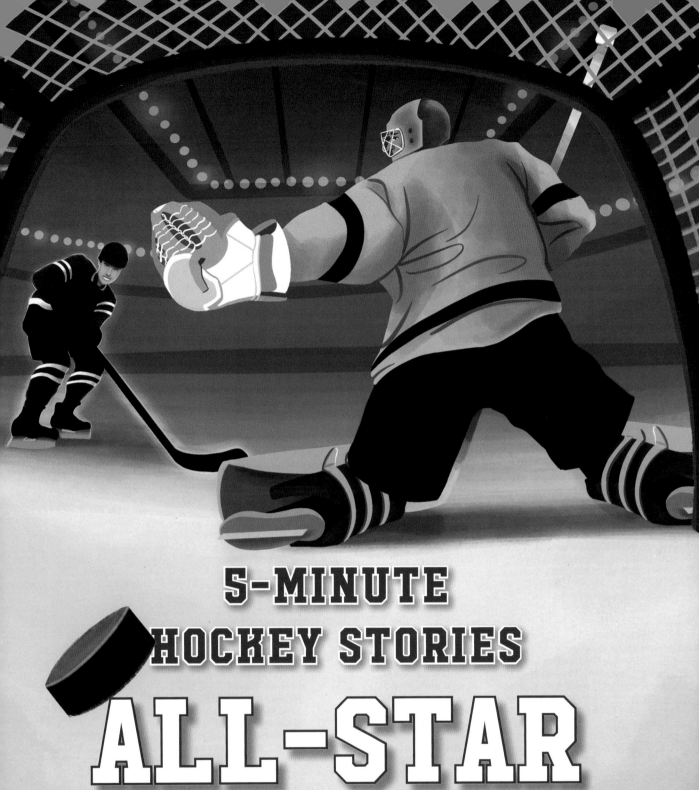

5-MINUTE HOCKEY STORIES
ALL-STAR EDITION

BY PETER NORMAN · ILLUSTRATED BY CHELSEA CHARLES

Collins

HarperCollins books may be purchased for educational, business, or sales promotional use through our Special
Markets Department.

HarperCollins Publishers Ltd
Bay Adelaide Centre, East Tower
22 Adelaide Street West, 41st Floor
Toronto, Ontario, Canada
M5H 4E3

www.harpercollins.ca

Library and Archives Canada Cataloguing in Publication

Title: 5-minute hockey stories / Peter Norman ; illustrations by Chelsea Charles.
Other titles: Five-minute hockey stories
Names: Norman, Peter, 1973- author. | Charles, Chelsea, 1994- illustrator.
Description: All star edition.
Identifiers: Canadiana 20240371666 | ISBN 9781443471770 (hardcover)
Subjects: LCSH: Hockey players—Biography—Juvenile literature. | LCSH: National Hockey League—
Juvenile literature. | LCGFT: Picture books. | LCGFT: Biographies.
Classification: LCC GV848.5.A1 N67 2024 | DDC j796.962092/2—dc23

Printed and bound in Malaysia
IMG

Contents

A LITTLE PLAYER WITH BIG DREAMS

Are you smaller than most people your age? Do you get picked last when captains choose teams? Do people tell you you'll never go far in sports? You don't need to listen to those people. Just ask Mitch Marner.

When he was a young player, hoping to earn a spot in the NHL, some people said he was too small to make it. Some said he was too weak.

But Mitch was determined to pursue his dream. Sometimes, along the way, he doubted himself. But he stuck with it, he practised endlessly, and he perfected his skills.

Not only did he make the NHL, he made it onto his favourite team. And, in 2022, he set an all-time team record.

One Saturday night in Tampa Bay, the Lightning were facing the Toronto Maple Leafs. Early in the second period, a Toronto player took a penalty.

When Mitch stepped onto the ice, he didn't expect to score. This was a penalty-killing shift.

When you kill a penalty, your most important job is to play defence. The other team has an extra player on the ice, and you must do everything you can to stop them from scoring.

You might have to block a shot.
You might have to intercept a pass.
You might have to shoot the puck out of your zone.

If you're really lucky, you might get the puck and carry it into the opposing zone. The other team will have to chase you, wasting their power-play time.

But you probably won't score a goal. Short-handed goals are rare.
All season long, Mitch Marner had been killing penalties.
He blocked shots.
He intercepted passes.
He shot the puck out of his zone.
But, all season long, Mitch hadn't scored a short-handed goal.

The Leafs sent the puck down the ice. A Lightning defenceman picked it up behind his net and started up the ice. He passed the puck back to a player behind him.

The problem was, there was no player behind him. He passed it to no one!

Mitch saw his chance. He rushed forward and stole the loose puck. Then he swooped to his right, crossing in front of Tampa Bay goalie Andrei Vasile-vskiy, who fell forward onto his belly.

Here was Mitch's chance for a goal! He shot . . .

. . . and he missed.

But his quick, unexpected play had surprised the Tampa Bay players. As they scrambled to get into defensive position, the puck went back to Mitch's teammate, who passed it in front of the net.

Mitch was waiting there, and he scooped the puck past Vasilevskiy. A short-handed goal!

This was no ordinary short-handed goal either. This was a record-breaking goal.

9

For weeks, Mitch had been on a hot streak. He had scored a goal or assist in every single game for eighteen games in a row. And this was game number nineteen. It was the first time a Maple Leaf had scored points in nineteen straight games.

Mitch was born and grew up in the Toronto area, and he had cheered for the Leafs his whole life. So he was very proud to wear that big blue maple leaf. And now he had a team record.

The Toronto Maple Leafs are a very old team. They have played under three different names. First they were the Toronto Arenas. Then they were the Toronto St. Patricks. Then, finally, they changed their name to the Toronto Maple Leafs. When Mitch played his first game as a Leaf, the team was almost one hundred years old!

One hundred years is a very long time. But in all that time, no other Maple Leafs player had done what Mitch did.

He didn't stop there. Three days later, he had an assist against the Dallas Stars. His point streak was extended to twenty games.

Two days after that, a goal against the Los Angeles Kings. Twenty-one games.

Two days after that, a goal and an assist against the Calgary Flames. Twenty-two games.

Three days later, in a 7–0 win against the Anaheim Ducks, Mitch got two assists. His streak ended there, at twenty-three games.

Today, nobody talks about how small Mitch Marner is. They talk about how big he is—he's one of the biggest stars in Maple Leafs history.

MICHIGAN!

The score was 0–0. Each team had taken seven shots on goal, but no one had beaten the goalies yet. Getting that first goal was going to take something special.

Trevor Zegras was a rookie on the Anaheim Ducks. This was only his forty-ninth game in the NHL. The Ducks were in Buffalo, playing the Sabres. His teammates carried the puck into the offensive zone, and he went behind the net. He knew how to do some pretty cool things from back there. Maybe he could do something special now.

Ducks winger Rickard Rakell skated to the puck in the corner and backhanded a pass to Trevor. Trevor took the puck on his stick and scanned the front of the net.

17

One Duck stood in front—Sonny Milano. Maybe Trevor could pass the puck to him, but that might be tricky. All five Sabres skaters were standing in front of the goal, ready to check Sonny if he got the puck.

And then, over the noise of skates and sticks and voices, Trevor heard Sonny shout one word:

"Michigan!"

The Michigan is a very difficult type of goal. To score a Michigan, you have to imitate a lacrosse player, using the blade of your stick to lift the puck in the air before releasing it into the net.

Of course, a lacrosse player has a huge advantage that a hockey player doesn't—at the end of the lacrosse stick is a little net that cradles the ball. To pull off this move, a hockey player must balance the puck flat on the blade of the stick.

It's really, really hard.

Why do we call it a "Michigan"? Because the first one was scored by a University of Michigan forward named Mike Legg, back in 1996.

But it took more than fifteen years for an NHL player to make a successful attempt at this difficult move. In 2019, Andrei Svechnikov of the Carolina Hurricanes did it twice.

And now, a young rookie for the Ducks was ready to do it again.

Except, this time, something strange happened.

Trevor Zegras didn't score.

When Sonny Milano shouted "Michigan," he expected to see Trevor lift the puck, swoop it around the front of the net on the blade of his stick, and then release it high over the goalie's shoulder into the top of the net.

Not this time. Trevor had an even more creative idea.

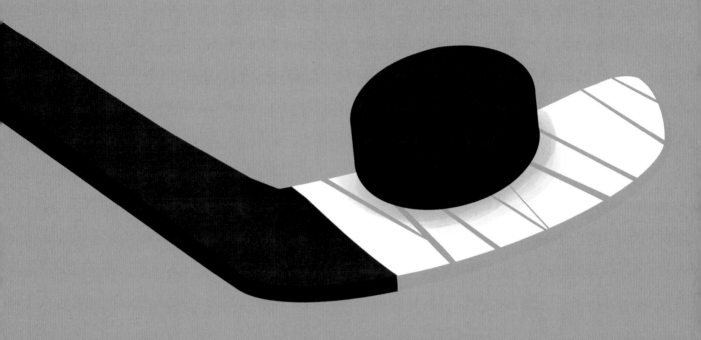

He pressed the blade of his stick overtop of the puck, then quickly flipped it to balance the puck on his blade.

So far, so good.

Then he raised his blade into the air, with the puck resting on top of it.

So far, still so good.

But he did not wrap it around the net. Instead, he flipped the puck into the air. It rose up, hovering, then fluttered down in front of Sonny. Sonny raised his stick and tapped the puck past a bewildered goalie.

Trevor didn't score a Michigan goal . . . he scored a Michigan assist! "Are you kidding me?" shouted the TV announcer.

Trevor was as surprised as anyone. As Sonny skated toward him to celebrate, Trevor's mouth dropped open in astonishment, and his hands flew up to grip the top of his head.

After the game, an interviewer asked him, "Is that the favourite goal you've been a part of in your entire life?"

Trevor grinned. "One hundred percent."

If you manage to score a one-of-a-kind Michigan assist, why not score a Michigan goal as well? Just fifteen games later, Trevor did exactly that.

The Ducks were in Montreal to play the Canadiens, and were already leading 3–1 in the second period. Trevor got possession of the puck to the goalie's left, skated smoothly behind the net, and without missing a stride, raised the puck up and over the goalie's right shoulder.

That was one of twenty-three goals Trevor scored that season. As one of the hottest young players in the league, he finished second for the Calder Trophy for rookie of the year, and he was selected to appear with Sarah Nurse on the cover of the *NHL 23* video game.

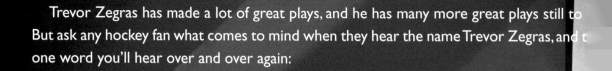

Trevor Zegras has made a lot of great plays, and he has many more great plays still to
But ask any hockey fan what comes to mind when they hear the name Trevor Zegras, and t
one word you'll hear over and over again:

"Michigan!"

A GOLDEN RECORD

Today was the last hockey game Canada would play at the Beijing Olympics. The winner would receive the gold medal. The men's hockey team had been eliminated from their competition, so the women were the only Canadian team that could take home a medal.

Sarah Nurse was Canada's leading scorer. She was having a terrific tournament. In just six games, she had already scored four goals and twelve assists. That gave her sixteen points.

If she could get just one more, she would tie the record for the most points in one Olympic tournament. Sixteen years earlier, Hayley Wickenheiser, one of Sarah's hockey heroes growing up, had scored seventeen in Torino, Italy. No one else had equalled her record.

But Sarah was close.

Sarah wasn't focused on the scoring record, though. What she cared about was that gold medal. This was her second Olympics. Last time, Team Canada lost to the United States in the final game.

Sarah did not want to go home with a silver medal again, and she would do whatever she had to do to help her team win.

If that meant scoring points, she would score points.

And she did. In the first period, she deflected a shot from the point. It got past the goalie, hit one post, hit the other post, and went into the net. It was Sarah's fifth goal and seventeenth point of the tournament, tying Hayley's record.

And then, in the second period, she assisted on a goal by Marie-Philip Poulin. That was her eighteenth point. Sarah had set a new record!

And Canada had a 3–0 lead over their American rivals.

The game wasn't over yet, though. The US stormed back with two more goals, and it was a tense final few minutes for Team Canada. But they held on for the victory.

Beating the scoring record was something to be proud of. Winning gold was a phenomenal feeling. But for Sarah, the victory was about more than points and medals.

When Sarah was three years old, her dad took her to the skating rink for the first time. He was from Trinidad. He had not grown up playing hockey, but he loved sports, and he believed it was important for a Canadian kid to learn to skate.

Not only was her dad athletic, her whole family was athletic. Sarah had uncles who played professional football. One of her cousins, Kia, would grow up to play basketball at the Olympics. Another cousin, Darnell, would play more than five hundred games for the Edmonton Oilers.

But Sarah was a girl, and some people felt girls weren't "real" hockey players. When she heard a coach say to a boy, "Don't play like a girl," it made her mad. She was a great hockey player. Boys should try to play like her!

Also, Sarah did not know many other Black girls who played hockey. Some people thought she didn't belong in hockey just because of the colour of her skin. It made Sarah really mad when people told her she should play basketball instead.

Those people were wrong, of course. Sarah definitely belonged in hockey. But she wanted to prove it.

"If I want them to shut up," she told herself, "I have to beat them on the ice."

And she did. In fact, she became one of the greatest players in the history of women's hockey, and her record-breaking performance in Beijing was all the proof she needed. Sarah became the first Black woman to win a gold medal in Olympic hockey.

Sarah knew that some things in life are more important than sports. She made a promise to herself. She would do her very best at playing hockey, but she would also do her very best to encourage girls and Black people and anyone else who might feel excluded from the sport. She made it her mission to fight against the kind of prejudice she faced as a girl.

In 2022, the same year as her record-breaking Olympics, Sarah made a big step forward for girls and women in hockey.

For more than thirty years, the popular video game NHL had featured only men on its cover. That changed with *NHL 23*. Now, girls playing their favourite video game see two famous players on the cover. One of them is Trevor Zegras. The other is Sarah Nurse.

What's that red-and-black jersey she's wearing? It's her Team Canada uniform. The same colours she wore proudly that sunny Thursday in Beijing, when she broke the Olympic record and finally won gold.

THE SHUTOUT KING

If you're a hockey forward, you may dream of scoring the big goal that wins a championship. Maybe in overtime, like Sidney Crosby and Marie-Philip Poulin did at the Olympics.

But if you're a goalie, you're unlikely to score a goal. Your dream is a bit different. Maybe it's to make a big save in the final game of a playoff series. Maybe even to allow zero goals all game, winning the series with a shutout.

That would be wonderful. A dream come true. Now imagine doing it five times in a row.

In the last game of the Stanley Cup Final in 2020, Andrei Vasilevskiy of the Tampa Bay Lightning achieved what many goalies dream of—a shutout to win the Stanley Cup.

He stopped the puck with his pads, with his stick, with his blocker, with his gloves. He stopped the puck standing up, kneeling, even sitting down.

Not a single puck got into the net.

At the other end of the ice, his teammates scored twice. When the final buzzer sounded, they raced down the ice to embrace him. The Lightning were Stanley Cup champions. And so was Andrei Vasilevskiy.

He learned to play goalie from his father, also named Andrei, who played in the Russian Superleague for almost twenty years. Andrei Sr. never had the chance to play for a Stanley Cup, and he was proud to see his son earn one with a shutout.

The next year, Andrei won thirty-two games for the Lightning and earned five regular-season shutouts. He was named a First Team All-Star. The Lightning qualified for the playoffs and prepared to defend their title.

Their first opponent was the high-scoring Florida Panthers. The Lightning won the first two games, but the Panthers won two of the next three. In Game 6, Andrei stopped every shot he faced—twenty-nine in total, including five from very close to the net. Tampa Bay won the game and the series. Andrei had won two consecutive playoff series with shutouts.

Next up, the Carolina Hurricanes. This series was over in five games, and Andrei won the last game with another twenty-nine-save shutout. His series-winning shutout streak was up to three.

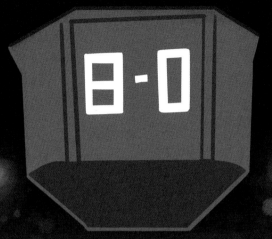

The semifinal series against the New York Islanders was wild. With the series tied 2–2, Andrei got another shutout in an 8–0 blowout, but the Islanders won the next game in overtime. So the series would have to be decided in Game 7.

All game long, the Lightning were able to score only one goal against Islanders goalie Semyon Varlamov. But that was enough to win the game, because Andrei got another shutout. He had won four series in a row with shutouts.

Now the Lightning were going to the Stanley Cup Final. Could they defend their championship and win the Cup two years in a row?

To do that, they would have to defeat Nick Suzuki and the Montreal Canadiens.

In the first three games, Montreal was able to score only five goals against Andrei—Nick Suzuki got two of them—and Tampa Bay went up 3–0 in the series. An overtime win for the Canadiens in Game 4 forced a fifth game. But that was as far as the series would go.

In Game 5, Andrei's teammates scored just one goal against Canadiens goalie Carey Price, but it was all they needed. Why?

You guessed it. Another shutout.

Montreal tried hard to get the tying goal, but Andrei saved every single shot. With seconds left in the third period, his teammates cleared the puck out of the defending zone, the buzzer sounded, and the Tampa Bay Lightning had repeated as Stanley Cup champions.

Andrei Vasilevskiy had earned his fifth consecutive series-winning shutout. After the game, he was awarded the Conn Smythe Trophy as the best player in the playoffs. Even on a team loaded with stars like Steven Stamkos, Nikita Kucherov, and Victor Hedman, Andrei's play was so outstanding that he was the MVP.

Some players are famous for speed or scoring. Some players are famous for checking or blocking or passing. Andrei Vasilevskiy is famous for great saves.

And in those five remarkable series-clinching games, he saved every single shot he faced.

BEST BIRTHDAY EVER

Happy birthday, Gabe!"

Gabe sat up, rubbed his eyes, and looked around. His parents were standing in the doorway. His mom was holding a box covered in green wrapping paper with a white bow.

Green and white were Gabe's favourite colours. Why? Because of hockey.

Gabe was a hockey player, and he hoped to play in the NHL someday. His favourite NHL player was Jason Robertson of the Dallas Stars. Dallas's team colours were green and white.

Gabe had a green-and-white Jason Robertson jersey in his closet.

He had green-and-white Stars socks in his drawer.

He even had a green-and-white Stars toothbrush in the bathroom.

And now, as he sat up in bed and took the box his mother handed to him, he was wearing green-and-white Stars pyjamas.

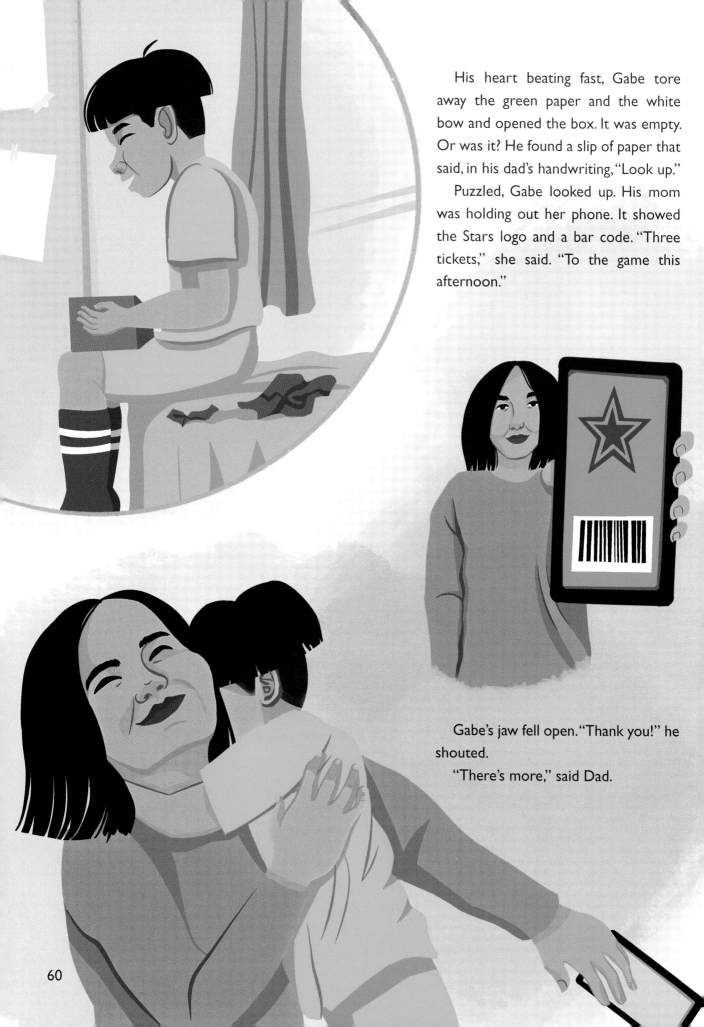

His heart beating fast, Gabe tore away the green paper and the white bow and opened the box. It was empty. Or was it? He found a slip of paper that said, in his dad's handwriting, "Look up."

Puzzled, Gabe looked up. His mom was holding out her phone. It showed the Stars logo and a bar code. "Three tickets," she said. "To the game this afternoon."

Gabe's jaw fell open. "Thank you!" he shouted.

"There's more," said Dad.

More? There was more? What could be more of a gift than Stars tickets?

"We have to get to the rink early," said Mom.

"Why?"

Mom smiled. "You'll see."

The morning dragged on. Gabe didn't know what to do with himself. He rearranged his hockey cards.

He watched Jason Robertson highlights. He ran up and down the stairs, just to get rid of his energy.

"I have an idea," said Mom after his fifth time up and down the stairs. She sat him at a table and brought him markers and sheets of paper. Dad found a book with pictures of international flags.

"Why don't you make a drawing of the Filipino flag?" said Mom.

Gabe was Filipino-American. His parents were born in the Philippines. He spoke English and loved American food, but he also loved Filipino food and the Filipino songs his parents taught him.

Jason Robertson was Filipino-American too. His mother was born in the Philippines and moved to Los Angeles when she was a young child. Like Gabe, he liked Filipino food and was interested in his mother's language and culture. And now he played on the Stars' number one line—and last season, he had become only the fourth Star in team history to score forty goals in a season. Around the world, young Filipino hockey fans cheered for him.

Gabe had no idea why his mom suggested he draw the flag, but once he got started it was kind of fun. He copied the shapes he saw in the book—a triangle on the left side, and inside that, a sun and three stars. Then he coloured it red, white, blue, and yellow.

Finally, it was time to go to the game! Gabe grabbed his green-and-white Stars jersey and his green and white Stars ball cap. "Grab that

At the rink, Gabe's parents didn't take him to his seat, or a hot dog stand, or a souvenir shop. They took him to a concrete corridor. "Why are we here?" asked Gabe.

He was expecting to hear "You'll see," but his parents were silent.

A door at the end of the corridor opened, and out came a man in shorts and a Stars ball cap. He saw Gabe's parents and waved.

For now, Gabe couldn't think. He couldn't speak. Jason Robertson was walking toward them, a big smile on his face. "You must be Gabe," he said.

Jason told Gabe he loved the flag he'd made.
"What's your favourite Filipino food?" Jason asked.
Gabe's answer was adobo.
"What's your favourite Filipino song?"
Gabe's answer was "Lagi."
"What's your favourite hockey team?"
I think you know what Gabe's answer was.

Jason signed Gabe's jersey, then returned to the dressing room to prepare for the game. Gabe sat in the stands and watched his favourite player. He cheered when Jason scored a goal in the second period. In the third period, Gabe munched on a hot dog with relish (green) and mayonnaise (white).

That night, after he had changed into his green-and-white pyjamas and brushed his teeth with the green-and-white toothbrush, his parents wished him good night.

Gabe was already half-asleep, sliding into dreams of whizzing along the ice like Jason Robertson. But he woke up just enough to say, "Thanks, Mom. Thanks, Dad. Best birthday ever."

THE FASTEST WOMAN IN THE WORLD

Kendall woke up. Outside, it was a sunny day in San Jose, California. Inside, her hotel room was dark. She opened the curtains.

She looked at her phone. Two missed calls. Who was trying to get hold of her so early in the morning?

A text came in. "I need you to pick up the phone," it said.

Kendall Coyne Schofield was in California for the NHL All-Star weekend. She was one of a group of women who had been chosen to play an exhibition game. The idea was to demonstrate how fast and skilled the women were, before the NHL All-Stars had their chance to show off.

That game had happened yesterday, and now Kendall was ready to relax, hang out, and watch some hockey. But first she had to answer this message. She dialled the number that had texted her.

"I hope you had a good sleep," said the voice on the other end of the line. It was one of the tournament organizers. "Because it's time to put your skates back on. We want you to compete in the Fastest Skater competition."

What on earth? Kendall didn't understand. The Fastest Skater competition was for NHL players. Why did they want her to take part?

The answer was that Nathan MacKinnon, who was supposed to skate in the competition, had a bruised foot. The tournament organizers knew Kendall was incredibly fast. So, they thought, why not ask her to replace Nathan?

Kendall grabbed her equipment and her Team USA jersey and hurried to the rink.

Fans crowded the seats. The best players in the NHL were skating around on the ice and sitting on the benches. Connor McDavid. Sidney Crosby. Andrei Vasilevskiy. TV cameras were everywhere.

The rink announcer told the crowd that it was time for the Fastest Skater competition. "First up," he boomed, "Kendall Coyne Schofield!" Fans in the crowd chanted, "USA! USA!"

Kendall grew up in Chicago. She was used to competing against boys. All through her childhood, she and her brother, Kevin, played sports and games together.

Their favourite was hockey. They spent so much time playing mini-sticks that the knees of their pants wore out!

She learned to skate when she was three, but it wasn't easy. She spent two years falling to the ice, getting back up, and falling down again. But she got better and better, and she fell down less and less.

"Don't fall." That's what she told herself now, at the centre red line in San Jose, with the fans chanting "USA."

Kendall leaned forward, resting her elbows on her knees, with her legs bent, ready to explode into action.

The whistle blew.

Kendall got her feet moving, fast. Her blades sliced into the ice as she built up momentum. In only three seconds, she had reached the first corner.

It's tricky to skate fast around a corner. As you lean to the side, you're likelier to fall. But Kendall handled the corner perfectly. She swooped behind the net and then around corner number two.

She charged back up the length of the ice, her ponytail streaming behind her. Her speed was more than thirty kilometres an hour.

Kendall had already won an Olympic gold medal. She had already won the Player of the Game award at the 4 Nations Cup. She had many trophies on her shelf. But now she was the first woman ever to participate in an NHL skills competition.

Two more corners, and Kendall was in the home stretch, sprinting back to the centre line. She leaned forward to make sure she crossed the line as soon as possible.

The arena erupted in applause as she finished the race. She had done a full lap of an NHL rink
in under fifteen seconds!

She skated past the benches, and the NHL All-Stars stood up, huge smiles on their faces, gloves raised to high-five her.

One of them was Connor McDavid, the fastest skater in the NHL. He was awestruck by Kendall's speed. "Wow!" he said. He ended up winning the competition, but he was less than one second faster than Kendall.

And what was Kendall's secret to getting around those corners so fast?

A TV announcer asked her that question after the event. "Just keep my feet moving, cross over," she said. And then, laughing, she revealed the most important secret of all. "Don't fall."

WHAT'S THAT NOISE?

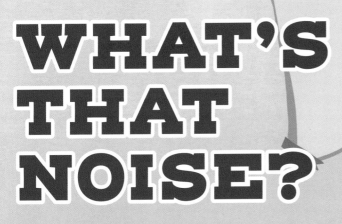

Taylor lined up her stuffed animals in a row, propping up mini hockey sticks to fit in their hands. Wham! From somewhere in the house came a sudden loud bang. Taylor paid it no attention.

Taylor was excited. Her friend Jen was coming over to play at Taylor's house for the first time. Taylor and Jen were in the same kindergarten class at their school in Cole Harbour, Nova Scotia. They liked stuffed animals, but what they liked even more was hockey. So Taylor had turned her animal collection into a hockey team.

Taylor placed a mini hockey helmet on top of her plush bunny rabbit, straightened the striped shirt on the panda referee, and went downstairs. Her mother was in the kitchen, putting cookies on a plate.

"Is it time yet, Mom?" Bam! Another enormous bang. But Taylor's mother didn't react to it. She just looked casually at her watch. "They should be here any minute."

The doorbell rang.

Taylor raced to the door. Jen was there, and while their mothers chatted, Taylor led her friend upstairs.

"Cool!" said Jen, looking at the array of animals with their mini hockey sticks.

Taylor grabbed the rabbit's stick from its paws. "Let's play mini-sticks!"

Smash!

Jen could not contain her curiosity. "Taylor, what's that noise?"

"What noise?"

Bang!

"That one."

"Oh." Taylor laughed. "I don't even notice it anymore. That's just my brother, Sid."

Jen had heard about Sid Crosby. He was a really good hockey player. He was in high school, and he played midget hockey against kids even older than himself.

"What is he doing?" Jen asked.

"Come on," said Taylor. "I'll show you."

They headed down to the main floor.

They started down a second set of stairs. Below them, Jen could see a basement. Light streamed through a window. In front of the window was a hockey net.

A puck sailed through the air and hit the crossbar. Ping! went the bar. It was pretty loud, but it wasn't the same booming sound Jen had heard earlier.

A puck sailed through the air and hit the crossbar. Ping! went the bar. It was pretty loud, but it wasn't the same booming sound Jen had heard earlier.

Behind the net was a dryer made of white metal. Just your normal, everyday dryer. With one difference.

It was covered with black spots. It looked like someone had decided to paint it with polka dots—someone who wasn't very good at painting polka dots. The marks were scattered unevenly over the surface. Some of them were dots, but others were more like smears.

Kaboom!

Another puck rocketed across the basement. This one missed the net and slammed into the dryer, leaving a fresh black mark.

"Hey, Sid!" shouted Taylor. "Stop shooting! We're coming down!"

She led Jen to the bottom of the steps. At the far end of the basement stood Sid. He was wearing his hockey jersey and a friendly smile.

"This is my friend Jen," said Taylor.

"Hi, Jen," said Sidney. "How's it going?"

"What are you doing?" asked Jen, eyes wide.

Sid shrugged. "Shooting practice."

"Why are you shooting at your dryer?"

Sid laughed. "I'm not trying to hit the dryer. That's what happens when I miss the net."

"But I've heard of you. You're really good! How can you miss so much?"

"Nobody hits every shot." Sid chuckled again. "And I take a lot of shots."

All afternoon, as Taylor and Jen played mini-sticks upstairs, the puck continued banging on the dryer in the basement.

Taylor and Sidney both continued playing hockey. Taylor played on her university team as a goalie. Sidney became a pro. In fact, he became one of the best players in history. He won three Stanley Cups.

Sure, he still missed shots, just like he used to in his basement. But when it was really, really important, he didn't miss often. He scored one of the most famous goals of all time, the overtime gold-medal winner for Team Canada at the Olympics in Vancouver.

As for the dryer, it became pretty famous too. It even became a TV star. Sid and his Pittsburgh Penguins teammate Max Talbot starred in a commercial where they tried to shoot pucks into the dryer's open door.

Today, you can see it for yourself. In the Nova Scotia Sport Hall of Fame, among the trophies and sticks and jerseys you'd expect to see in a museum like that, the dryer is on display, proudly showing off those thick, black scuff marks from all the shots Sidney missed.

Back then, Taylor realized that even the best players miss some shots. But they keep on trying until they improve. Her brother was one of those players. Sid just wouldn't quit.

MOOSUM AND THE WILLOW BRANCH

When Fred Sasakamoose was five years old, he lived with his parents and brother and sisters in a small log cabin.

There was no electricity, but the children stayed warm in the clothes and blankets their mother made. At night, they got light from an oil lamp.

There was no fridge in the cabin or grocery store nearby, but their father hunted and fished, and their mother grew potatoes, turnips, and carrots, and she also picked berries.

There were no taps or running water, but there was a natural pond near the cabin. In the spring, summer, and fall, the family took water from the pond. In the winter, when it turned to ice, they brought snow into the cabin and melted it.

One day, their grandfather—or moosum, in the Cree language the Sasakamoose family spoke—came to live in the log cabin too.

He had a red beard and was so strong that he could lift the front end of a horse off the ground. He could not hear, and he could not speak. But he was able to teach the children all kinds of things just by showing them what to do. He taught Fred and his brother to fish and hunt, and how to track wild animals by studying their footprints.

This was the 1930s in Saskatchewan, and life was changing fast, especially for Indigenous families. But their moosum was able to show the children many aspects of their people's heritage. He built a Sweat Lodge, a place where the family could go to heal and worship.

One winter day, when the pond was frozen and snow was thick on the ground, Fred's moosum helped him get dressed. He put five pairs of socks on Fred's feet, then slid Fred's moccasins over them.

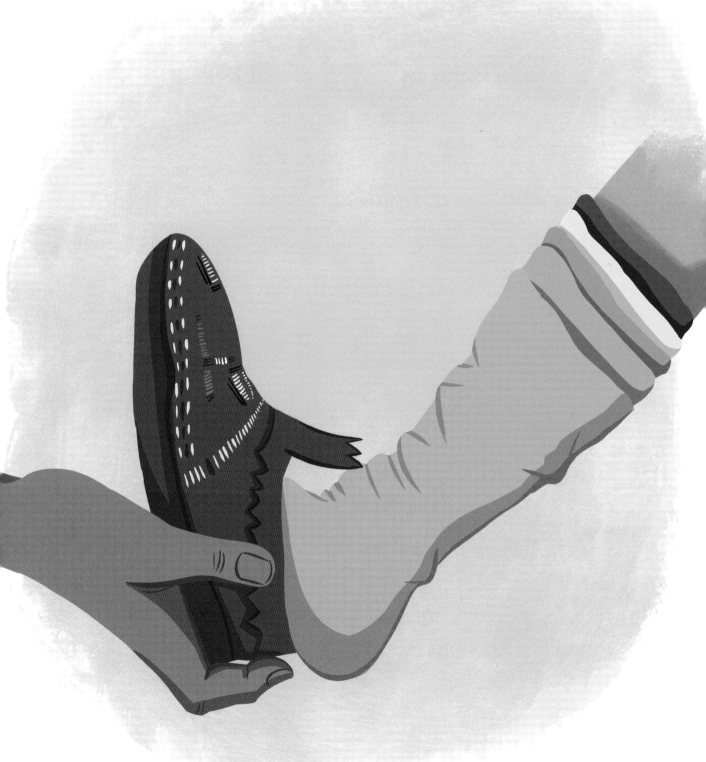

He took Fred outside, lifted him onto the sled, and pulled it down to the pond. From the back of the sled, he produced two skates. Fred's moosum put them onto Fred's feet.

Fred's feet were feeling pretty heavy. Each foot was wearing five socks, one moccasin, and one skate!

Fred's moosum lifted him up in the air and then set him down on the ice.

Fred didn't know what to do. He moved his feet. They flew out from under him, and he fell down.

His moosum picked him up and put his feet back on the ice.

Fred moved his feet again. Again they slid out from under him.

Again, his moosum set him on his feet.

Day after day, Fred and his moosum went to the pond. If there was snow on the ice, his moosum would shovel it off. If it was especially cold, he would build a small fire at the edge of the pond.

Soon, Fred could go several strides without falling. Then he could stay on his feet from one end of the pond to the other. When he didn't need to be picked up from the ice anymore, his moosum cut a hole in the ice, sat on a bucket, and fished.

One afternoon, his moosum got an idea. He walked into a stand of trees and came out a few moments later with a long willow branch.

That night, in the glow of the oil lamp, he took a knife and worked on that branch. Under the blade of his knife, it grew smoother and smoother. Then he took one end of the branch and bent it.

107

The next day, at the pond, he handed the branch to Fred. It was Fred's first hockey stick!

Then Fred's moosum found a piece of frozen cow poop. He tossed it onto the ice. It wasn't rubber, and it wasn't perfectly round, but it would make a pretty good puck.

And that's how Fred Sasakamoose first began to learn hockey.

When he was still a teenager, Fred became one of the first Indigenous players in the NHL. He played eleven games for the Chicago Black Hawks—and although he didn't score, he came close. He had a hard, fast slap shot that some of the biggest stars in the NHL admired—and feared! You didn't want to be standing in the way when Fred let his slap shot fly.

After he retired from hockey, he worked with children who wanted to play sports. He helped set up an Indigenous hockey league. For a while, he was Chief of the Ahtahkakoop Cree Nation. He is honoured in several halls of fame.

Fred Sasakamoose achieved many things on the ice, and off. But it all began one cold afternoon, on a frozen pond beside a log cabin, with a willow branch and a frozen cow patty, and his moosum watching from the shore.

THE SHOOTING STAR

Both teams have played a great game. The crowd has been yelling and clapping and chanting all night. But when the final buzzer sounds, the score is tied. There's no winner. We need overtime.

In the NHL regular season, overtime lasts five minutes. But if nobody scores in those five minutes, it's time to try something else.

Shootout!

One after the other, players from each team skate in alone on the goalie. A pure contest between the shooter and the goaltender. It's a lot of pressure!

But some players love the pressure of the shootout. Some take the chance to show their most spectacular moves, bringing the fans to their feet.

In his fourth NHL season, Nick Suzuki of the Montreal Canadiens became one of those players. His first chance came in early November, in Detroit, against the Red Wings. He skated slowly down the right wing, then cut across the ice toward the net. He lowered his shoulder as if he were going to shoot at the right side of the net, then stickhandled rapidly and shot the puck into the other side.

"Great move!" shouted his teammates as he skated past the bench, fist-bumping them.

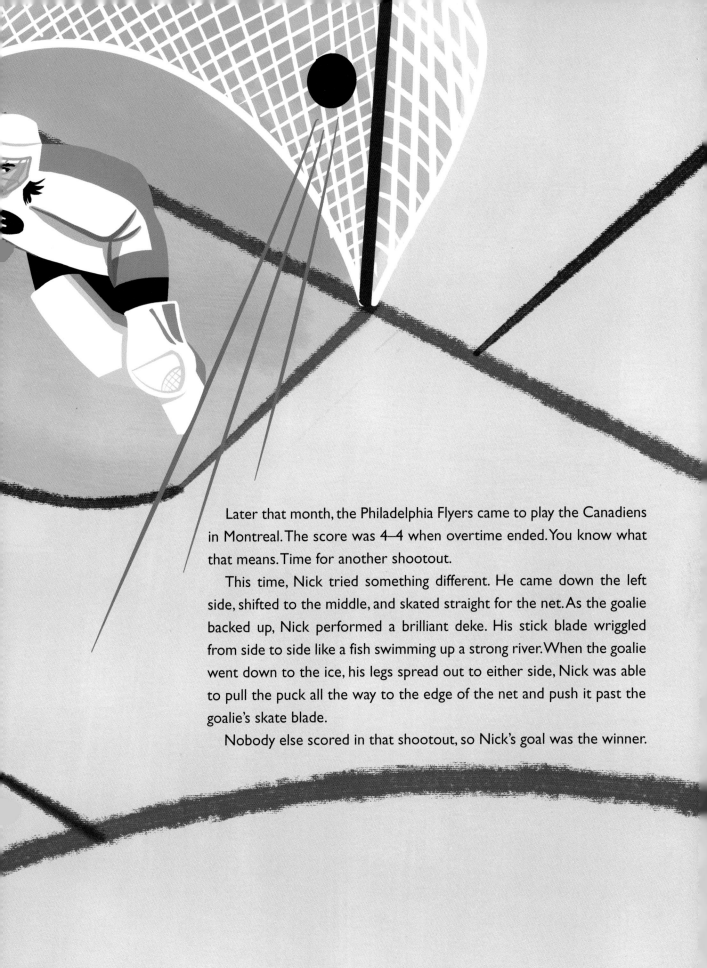

Later that month, the Philadelphia Flyers came to play the Canadiens in Montreal. The score was 4–4 when overtime ended. You know what that means. Time for another shootout.

This time, Nick tried something different. He came down the left side, shifted to the middle, and skated straight for the net. As the goalie backed up, Nick performed a brilliant deke. His stick blade wriggled from side to side like a fish swimming up a strong river. When the goalie went down to the ice, his legs spread out to either side, Nick was able to pull the puck all the way to the edge of the net and push it past the goalie's skate blade.

Nobody else scored in that shootout, so Nick's goal was the winner.

Six days later, the Canadiens travelled to Chicago for a game with the Blackhawks. This time, the shooters, not the goalies, were the stars of the shootout. Five goals were scored on six tries. Only one player missed his shot. Do you think it was Nick?

You're right. Of course it wasn't Nick.

He used a move like the one he'd done in Detroit, but this time he shot the puck into the opposite side of the net.

Goalies study the best players on other teams, getting to know their favourite moves, learning what to expect when they face those players. But how could they figure out what Nick would do in a shootout? Whatever they'd seen him do before, he was going to do in a slightly different way the next time.

Before the end of the year, Nick had one more shootout magic trick to perform, this time against the Calgary Flames.

You know how it's impossible to predict what Nick will do? Well, that's kind of a trick too.

The Flames goalie probably figured Nick would not do what he did last time. And guess what? Nick did exactly the same thing as last time.

As the puck fluttered past the goalie into the left side of the net, he threw his hands to his head in dismay. He couldn't believe he'd been fooled!

The Canadiens won the shootout again. They had a perfect record—four wins and no losses in the shootouts so far that season. And Nick had a perfect record—four shots, four goals.

As the Canadiens players celebrated New Year's, Nick had a lot to be proud of. He was the youngest captain in Canadiens history. He was a star player on an exciting young team. And he'd thrilled Montreal fans with something magic—his shootout wizardry.

As for his streak, it wasn't over yet. In March, against the Carolina Hurricanes, another fantastic deke would extend his run of shootout goals to five in a row. Finally, two days later, New York Rangers goalie Igor Shesterkin thwarted Nick's next attempt and ended the streak at five.

Imagine you're an NHL goalie. Both teams have played a great game. The fans have yelled and clapped and chanted all night. But overtime ends, and the score is tied.

You take a drink from your water bottle. You look up the ice to see who's shooting first.

Uh-oh. It's Nick Suzuki.

What will he do? What move will he use this time? You simply can't be sure.

But whatever he does, it'll probably be magic.

CAPTAIN CLUTCH

Marie-Philip Poulin and her teammates walked through a dim tunnel. They could hear a low mumble—thousands of hockey fans in their seats, waiting for the team to come out.

As the players stepped into the bright arena, the crowd roared. Most of the fans were wearing Team Canada jerseys—Marie-Philip's team. Some of them leaned over the glass to give the players high-fives and fist bumps. The noise was incredible.

This was Vancouver, it was the 2010 Olympics, and it was the gold-medal game. Marie-Philip was only eighteen, but she had been named to the national team. All of her teammates were older, with more experience. But Marie-Philip knew she belonged. Only fourteen minutes into the game, she proved it.

As the first period got going, the other team, the United States, had some really good chances. But Canada's goalie, Shannon Szabados, made spectacular saves to keep the score 0–0.

With six minutes left, Marie-Philip's linemate, Jennifer Botterill, stole the puck in the US zone. Marie-Philip tapped her stick on the ice to let Jennifer know she was ready for a pass.

Jennifer sent the puck back to Marie-Philip, who whipped it at the net. The puck flew up . . . up . . . and over the goalie's arm. The first goal of the game!

Just three minutes later, she scored again. That was the last goal of the game—Marie-Philip was the only skater who could beat the goalies all night. At the final buzzer, as the crowd roared, Marie-Philip and her teammates leapt off the bench to celebrate an Olympic gold medal.

Because the US scored zero goals, Marie-Philip's first goal was the game-winner—the one goal Canada needed to outscore the other team.

If you like math, you can figure out which goal is the winning goal in any game. First, you take the number of goals the losing team scored. Then you add one. This time, the losing team scored zero. What's zero plus one? It's one. So Canada's first goal, goal number one, was the winner.

And it was scored by the youngest player!

Four years later, she did it again.

Canada versus the US for Olympic gold. Marie-Philip scored in the last minute to tie the game. Overtime was fast and action-packed, with more great saves by goalie Shannon Szabados. And can you guess who finally scored?

That's right, it was Marie-Philip. Her goal ended one of the most dramatic hockey games anyone has ever seen.

Marie-Philip was so important to Team Canada that they named her team captain in 2014. At the World Championship in 2021, she scored another overtime goal to win the tournament.

Some players are very, very good at scoring goals when it matters most. We call them clutch players. Marie-Philip was the ultimate clutch player. She now had three gold-medal-winning goals at the Olympic and World Championship tournaments. Nobody else has done that. Not in hockey. Not in soccer. Not in any sport!

Plus she was team captain. So people began to call her Captain Clutch.

In 2022, it was time for the Winter Olympics again. As usual, Canada played the US for the gold. Also as usual, Captain Clutch scored the most important goal.

In the first period, Marie-Philip scored to give Canada a 2–0 lead. In the second period, Marie-Philip scored again.

But the US did not give up. Soon, they made it 3–1. Then, with a couple of minutes left in the game, the American team pulled their goalie. It was going to be another dramatic finish.

But then, disaster. At centre ice, Marie-Philip collided with a US player, and the referee's arm went up in the air. Penalty!

Captain Clutch was going to have to watch from the penalty box. She banged her glove on the glass to encourage her teammates.

What she couldn't do was go out on the ice to help kill the penalty. The US scored on the power play. It was 3–2.

Only 13.5 seconds were left on the clock. Could Captain Clutch and her teammates hold on to the lead?

Marie-Philip took the faceoff at centre ice. She sent the puck down the ice. The US brought it back the other way, but the buzzer sounded, and Marie-Philip's teammates poured off the bench. They were Olympic champions again.

Oh, and the final score? Canada 3, USA 2. Canada's third goal, Marie-Philip's second, was the gold-medal winner. Unbelievable but true—she had scored the winner again.

If anyone ever deserved the nickname Captain Clutch, it's the magnificent Marie-Philip Poulin.

THE YOUNGEST LEADER

I f you like to watch hockey, you've probably seen Connor McDavid play. And if you've seen Connor play you've probably seen him do something amazing.

You've seen him skate faster than anyone else on the ice. You've seen him keep the puck on his stick with dazzling dekes that befuddle defencemen and turn goalies into human pretzels. You've seen him score stunning goals. You've seen him make jaw-dropping passes.

Connor McDavid knows what to do when he steps onto the ice. He plays with confidence and poise, looking as if nothing in the world could ever stop him. As if nothing could ever scare him.

But on this morning, Connor was nervous.

He was going to a meeting at the office of the general manager of his team, the man in charge of hiring coaches and players, making trades. The boss.

The manager was going to be there, but so was the coach. And an assistant coach. And another assistant coach. No one was telling him what the meeting was about.

Connor was only nineteen years old. He was about to start the second season of his NHL career. Why did they want to see him now? Was he in trouble?

But when he knocked on the door and opened it, and saw all those bosses standing in the office, waiting for him, it didn't look like he was in trouble at all. The manager and coaches were wearing big smiles.

Everyone knows that Connor is an excellent hockey player. Many people think he is the best hockey player in the world. But not many of us have met him and spent time with him.

People who know him can tell you something else about Connor McDavid—he's a humble, kind, hard-working person. That's what his teammates say. It's what his coaches say. Old friends say the same thing, and so do the families Connor stayed with when he was a teenager playing games far away from home.

When Connor played his first NHL game for the Edmonton Oilers, he was just eighteen. An injury prevented him from playing the full season, but when he did play, he was outstanding.

His teammates and coaches saw what a brilliant player he is—but they saw something else too. They saw what an impressive person he is.

And that's why, on this October afternoon, his bosses had asked him to come to the general manager's office. They had a special question for him. "Connor," said the manager, "will you be the team captain?"

Connor was stunned. This was a huge thing to ask of a nineteen-year-old.

A captain has to do many things other players don't have to do. It's not an easy job.

The captain sometimes has to talk to the referee about rules and penalties.

When there's a special faceoff or ceremony before the game, the captain is the one who participates.

The captain is expected to talk to news reporters and fans, answering their questions on behalf of the team.

And the captain is supposed to work hard every shift, showing the other players on the team the standard of play that is expected of them. This is called "leading by example."

These tasks require someone who's strong and brave, someone who has a positive attitude, someone who works hard, someone other people admire. Someone who has what hockey players call "character."

Usually, the captain is one of the older players on the team. That's true outside of hockey too—leaders are often older than the people they lead.

Do you have a younger brother or sister? Would you want them to be your boss? No? That's why leaders are often older.

Not Connor—he was the second-youngest player on the team. And he knew that it would be a tough job. But he knew how to play well, he knew how to lead by example. Connor was ready to wear that big letter C on his chest.

"Thank you," Connor said. "It's an honour. I'll do it."

Connor would go on to do many astonishing things. He would win scoring titles. He would set records. What he didn't know was that even now, just by saying yes, he had set a new all-time NHL record. Connor McDavid was the youngest captain in NHL history.

THE FROZEN TENNIS COURT

It was a dark, cold December morning in Toronto. The sun wasn't up yet, but streetlights shone on icy roads lined with snowbanks.

An SUV pulled into the parking lot of Wedgewood Park.
The doors opened, and out jumped three boys.
First out of the car was Quinn, the oldest—he was eight.

Next came his brother Jack, who was six.

And then, finally, four-year-old Luke. His mom had to help him down from the vehicle.

The boys could see their breath in the cold air as they chattered excitedly. Their mom helped them lug a bag of skates and equipment to a rink.

During the summer, this rink was a tennis court, but in the winter it was flooded with water and frozen.

This wasn't the kind of ice you see at NHL games. There, you'll see circles and dots to help the players and officials know where the puck should be dropped. You'll see red and blue lines that tell the players where they can take the puck, and when. You'll see boards around the ice to keep the players and puck from spilling into the seats.

Not here. Here, all you saw was plain, clear ice. No red lines. No blue lines. No circles or dots. There were white lines, though. They were part of the tennis court, and even in winter you could see them through the ice. Nothing to do with hockey!

With Mom's help, the brothers tied their skates, pulled on their gloves, and grabbed their sticks. Mom tossed a puck onto the ice, and they raced after it, Quinn in the lead, Jack close behind, little Luke falling down on his bum and then leaping quickly back to his feet to scramble after them.

Quinn, Jack, and Luke Hughes knew what it was like to play in a proper rink, with the lines and dots and boards. All three of them were hockey players.

They didn't just play hockey; they lived for hockey. They watched it. They studied it. Their mom had been a hockey player. Their dad had been a hockey player and now worked as a coach. Both parents taught them how to improve at the game.

Because of Dad's coaching jobs, the Hughes family moved around a lot.

When Quinn and Jack were born, they lived in Orlando, Florida. Luke was born in New Hampshire, where Dad worked for the Boston Bruins. And now they were in Toronto because Dad was an assistant coach for the Toronto Marlies.

No matter where they went, the Hughes brothers' hockey obsession followed. They joined leagues and became star players.

But when they came here, to the outdoor rink, they were free to play however they wanted. No refs. No rules. Pure freedom.

They got there early in the morning, before anyone else.

They had the entire sheet of ice to themselves.

They could skate in wild circles. They could pass the puck all the way from one end of the ice to the other. They could go as fast as they pleased.

The Hughes brothers loved to have contests of skill—who could skate faster, shoot harder, deke more cleverly. They were different ages, but they were all excellent players.

Sometimes Mom stood at the edge of the rink. Sometimes she strapped on her own skates and joined them. But mostly she loved to watch them racing around the ice. She loved to hear the sound of their skate blades in the silent morning in this quiet neighbourhood. She loved to see their breath hanging in the air.

At the end of their morning skate, exhausted, sweaty underneath their layers of warm clothes, the boys would pile back into the SUV and drive home to get ready for the day ahead.

School. Hockey practice. Maybe a game.

And then home to bed, dreaming of the next morning's adventures on the open ice.

Quinn, Jack, and Luke continued to grow and improve. When they were teenagers, each one of them was chosen by an NHL team in the first round of the draft—Quinn by the Vancouver Canucks, Jack and Luke by the New Jersey Devils.

And they did amazing things in front of thousands of fans, in huge rinks with boards and lines and circles and dots and referees. Their skill and determination led to dazzling plays in important games.

Why were they so good? Because of their lifelong passion and determination to play and improve at hockey.

But that didn't come from lines and rules and dots.

It came to life on a flooded tennis court, on cold winter mornings, as they skated and passed and deked and shrieked with joy, their breath hanging in the air.